*Commentary on
the Pymander*

By G. R. S. Mead

Copyright © 2021 Lamp of Trismegistus. All rights reserved. No part of this publication may be reproduced or transmitted in any form or by any means, electronic or mechanical, including photocopying, recording, or by any information storage and retrieval system, without permission in writing from Lamp of Trismegistus. Reviewers may quote brief passages.

ISBN: 978-1-63118-588-5

Esoteric Classics

Other Books in this Series and Related Titles

The Hymns of Hermes by G R S Mead (978-1-63118-405-5)

Clairvoyance and Psychic Abilities by A Besant &c (978-1-63118-403-1)

Gnosis of the Mind by G R S Mead (978-1-63118-408-6)

Rosicrucian Rules, Secret Signs, Codes and Symbols by various (978-1-63118-488-8)

An Outline of Theosophy by C W Leadbeater (978-1-63118-452-9)

Paracelsus, the Four Elements and Their Spirits by M P Hall (978-1-63118-400-0)

Essays on Ancient Magic by Helena P Blavatsky (978-1-63118-535-9)

Essays on the Esoteric Tradition of Karma by A Besant &c (978-1-63118-426-0)

The Use of Evil by Annie Besant (978-1-63118-532-8)

Occult Arts by William Q. Judge (978-1-63118-559-5)

The Alchemical Catechism of Paracelsus by Paracelsus (978-1-63118-513-7)

Alchemy in the Nineteenth Century by Helena P Blavatsky (978-1-63118-446-8)

Qabbalistic Teachings and the Tree of Life by M P Hall (978-1-63118-482-6)

The Historic, Mythic and Mystic Christ by Annie Besant (978–1–63118–533–5)

The Hidden Mysteries of Christianity by Annie Besant (978–1–63118–534–2)

The Brotherhood of Religions by Annie Besant (978–1–63118–563–2)

The Hymn of Jesus by G R S Mead (978-1-63118-492-5)

The Religion of Theosophy by Bhagwan Das (978–1–63118–565–6)

The Machinery of the Mind by Dion Fortune (978-1-63118-451-2)

Vision of the Spirit by C. Jinarajadasa (978-1-63118-560-1)

The Leadbeater Reader: A Selection of Occult Essays (978-1-63118-483-3)

Audio versions are also available on Audible, Amazon and Apple

Other Books in this Series and Related Titles

Hypnotism and Mesmerism by Annie Besant (978–1–63118–587–8)

Spirits of Various Kinds by Helena P Blavatsky (978–1–63118–586–1)

The Hidden Language of Symbolism by Annie Besant (978–1–63118–585–4)

Eastern Magic & Western Spiritualism by Henry S Olcott (978–1–63118–584–7)

Spiritual Progress and Practical Occultism by H P Blavatsky (978–1–63118–583–0)

Memory and Consciousness by Besant & Blavatsky (978–1–63118–582–3)

The Origin of Evil by Helena P Blavatsky (978–1–63118–581–6)

The Camp of Philosophy: Studies in Alchemy by Bloomfield (978–1–63118–580–9)

The Testaments of the Twelve Patriarchs (978–1–63118–579–3)

Occult or Exact Science? by Helena P Blavatsky (978–1–63118–578–6)

Occultism, Semi-Occultism & Pseudo Occultism by A Besant (978–1–63118–577–9)

The Fourth-Gospel and Synoptical Problem by G R S Mead (978–1–63118–576–2)

On the Bhagavad-Gita by T Subba Row &c (978–1–63118–575–5)

What Theosophy Does for Us by C W Leadbeater (978–1–63118–574–8)

Spiritual Life for Man by Annie Besant (978–1–63118–573–1)

The Mysteries by Annie Besant (978–1–63118–572–4)

Fundamental Ideas of Theosophy by Bhagwan Das (978–1–63118–571–7)

Dreams: What They Are and Caused by C W Leadbeater (978–1–63118–570–0)

Communication Between Different Worlds by Annie Besant (978–1–63118–569–4)

Animism, Magic and the Omnipotence of Thought by S Freud (978–1–63118–568–7)

Buddhism by F Otto Schrader (978–1–63118–567–0)

Audio versions are also available on Audible, Amazon and Apple

Table of Contents

Introduction...7

Commentary on the Pymander

Of Vision and Apocalypse...9
The *Corpus Hermeticum*...11
The Great and the Little Man...12
The Presence...13
The Vision of Creation...14
First Emanation: The Descent of the Logos...17
The Revelation of the Pleroma...18
God Desiring Himself...20
Second Emanation: Mind the Maker...22
Third Emanation: The Descent of Man...24
The First Men...26
To Increase and Multiply...27
Love as the Will of God...28
The Way of Deathlessness...29
The Ascent of the Soul...30
The Eighth Sphere...31
Thrice-Greatest Hermes...33
The Spread of the Gnosis...36
The Meaning of "Pymander"...37
Conclusion...39

INTRODUCTION

The word "esoteric" can be difficult to define. Esotericism in general can be seen less as a system of beliefs and more as a category, which encompasses numerous, different systems of beliefs. It's a bit of juxtaposition, since the word "esoteric" indicates something that few people know about, while the term itself broadly covers numerous philosophies, practices, areas of study and belief systems.

In a greater sense, Esotericism acts as a storehouse for secret knowledge, which is often considered ancient (by *tradition, if not by fact),* passed down from generation to generation, in private. At various times in history, simply possessing the knowledge of some of these subjects, was considered illegal and a jailable offence, if discovered. This usually included such general topics as Alchemy, Pharmacology, Qabalah, Hermeticism, Occultism, Ceremonial Magic, Astrology, Divination, Rosicrucianism and so on. Collectively, these areas of study were often referred to as the esoteric sciences.

Sometimes, the outer garment of a subject isn't esoteric, while what is hidden beneath it, is. As an example, Freemasonry isn't necessarily esoteric by nature (at *least not anymore),* but certain signs, passwords and handshakes given to the candidate during their initiation, are in fact, esoteric, in the sense that they are hidden from the general public.

Today, in the twenty-first century, such topics are readily available at bookstores across the country, and numerous mainsteam publishers offer beginners guides and coffee-table volumes on many of these subjects, intended for mass appeal. Books like *"The Secret"* have turned previously arcane topics into household knowledge. All that being the case, however, it isn't to say that there still aren't buried secrets to uncover, ancient wisdom being ignored and forgotten mysteries to be explored. In fact, it is often that we are only able to further our own studies by standing on the shoulders of these disappearing giants.

Lamp of Trismegistus is doing its part to help preserve humanity's esoteric history by making some of these classics available to those students who are seeking to unearth the knowledge of these ancient colossi.

So, be sure to check other titles from our *Esoteric Classics* series, as well as our *Occult Fiction, Theosophical Classics, Foundations of Freemasonry Series, Supernatural Fiction, Paranormal Research Series, Studies in Buddhism* and our *Christian Apocrypha Series.* You can also download the audio versions of most of these titles from Amazon, Apple or Audible, for learning on the go.

COMMENTARY ON THE PYMANDER (POEMANDRES)

OF VISION AND APOCALYPSE

The Pymander treatise not only belongs to the most important type of the literature attributed to Hermes Trismegistus but is also the most important document within that type. It constitutes, so to speak, the Ground Gospel of the Hermetic Communities, in the form of a revelation or apocalypse received by the founder of the tradition. That founder, however, is not so much a historical personage as the personification of a teaching-power or grade of spiritual illumination -- in other words, of one who had reached the Hermetic or rather "Thrice-greatest" state of consciousness or enlightenment.

This stage of enlightenment is characterized by a heightening of the spiritual intuition that made the mystic capable of receiving the first touch of cosmic consciousness, and of retaining it in his physical memory when he returned to the normal state. The setting forth of the divine teaching is thus naturally in the form of apocalyptic scenes but of an ordered and logical nature. The treatise purports to be a setting forth of the spiritual "Epopteia" ("seeing beyond") of the Inner Mysteries, the Vision revealed by the Great Initiator or Master Hierophant, the One Mind of all-masterhood.

This Vision, as we are told by many seers and prophets of the time, was incapable of being set forth by "tongue of flesh" in its own proper terms, since it transcended the consciousness of normal humanity. Being in itself a living potent, intelligible reality, apart from all forms either material or intellectual in any way known to man, it pervaded his very being and made his whole nature respond to a new key of truth, or rather, vibrate in a higher octave so to say, where all things while remaining the same, received a new interpretation and intensity.

The interpretation of this Vision, however, was conditioned by the "matter" of each seer; he it: was who had to clothe the naked beauty of the Truth -- as the Gnostic Marcus would have phrased it -- with the fairest: garment he himself possessed: the highest thoughts, the best science, the fairest traditions, the most grandiose imagination known to him. Thus it is that we have so many modes of expression among the mystics, so many varieties of spiritual experience -- not because the experience itself was "other;" the experience was the "same" for all -- but the describing of it was conditioned by the religious, philosophical, and scientific background of the seer.

This element, then, is the basic fact in all such apocalyptic vision. It is, however, seldom that we meet with a document that has come to us straight from the hand of a seer writing down his own immediate experience without admixture of the personal viewpoint. For the delight of this Vision is not that it gave new facts or ideas of the same nature as those already in circulation, but that it threw light on existing traditions, and showed them forth as being parts of a whole. Once a man had come into touch with the Great Synthesis, there rushed into his mind innumerable passages of scripture, scraps of myths, fragments of cosmogenesis, facts, and symbols of all kinds that fitted naturally. These were not any special writer's monopoly, there was no copyright in them, and they were all utterances of the same Logos, the Great Instructor of humanity.

THE CORPUS HERMETICUM

Thus the literature that was produced in the *Corpus Hermeticum* was anonymous or pseudographic. There was first of all a nucleus of personal vision and direct illumination, then a grouping of similar matter from various sources into a whole for didactic purposes. Nor was there any idea among these mystics and scripture-writers that the form once issued should become forever stereotyped as infallible; there were many recensions and additions and interpolations. It was left to those without the sense of illumination to stereotype the forms and claim for them the infallacy of verbal dictation by the Deity. Those who wrote the apocalypses from personal knowledge of vision could not make such claim for their scriptures, for they *knew* how they were written and the nature of their hearing and sight at the time they were experienced.

Traditionally, we have to treat all such documents as natural human compositions, analyzing them with microscopic attention as literary compositions put together from other sources, overwritten, redacted, and interpolated. On the other hand, we have also to bear in mind that this was not done by clever manipulators and literary charlatans, but by men who regarded such work as a sacred and spiritual task, who endeavored to arrange all under the inspiration of a sweet influence for good, who believed themselves under guidance in their selection of matter, and in recombining the best in other scriptures into a new whole that might prove still better for the purpose of further enlightenment more suitable to their readers.

THE GREAT AND THE LITTLE MAN

The treatise begins with a deep meditation. By opening himself, the disciple reaches the consummation of his efforts, and receives initiation from the Master of the masters, who is to confer upon him authority to teach, that is, to be a master or like Hermes. That this Grand Master of the Inner Mysteries was both Man and Shepherd of men, the true Self of men, has been amply shown in the Prolegomena to the *Corpus Hermeticum*, but the striking parallelism with the very wording of our text, the Great Man, the "Being more than vast", who tells the little man, that though for the first time he now knows his Greater Self, that Self has always been "everywhere with you." This idea is best shown by the beautiful logos from the *Gospel of Eve* (presumably an early Egyptian gospel):

"I stood on a lofty mountain and saw a gigantic Man and another, a dwarf; and I heard, as it were, a voice of thunder, and drew nigh for to hear; and He spake unto me and said: I am thou, and thou art I; and wheresoever thou mayest be, I am there. In all am I scattered, and whencesoever thou willest, thou gatherest Me; and gathering Me, thou gatherest Thyself."

THE PRESENCE

The conditions of seeing the Holy Sight have been fulfilled by the disciple; he has weaned himself from all lower desires. No longer, like the theurgist in the Hermes-invocations of the popular cult, does he pray for wealth and fame and cheerful countenance, and the rest. His one desire, his only will, is now to "learn the things that are, and comprehend their nature and know God." He craves for Gnosis -- Gnosis of the Cosmos and its mysteries, Gnosis of Nature or the Great Mother, and, finally, Gnosis of God, the Father of the worlds. This is the one question he "holds in his mind." His whole being is concentrated into this question, this one point of interrogation.

It is to be noticed that we are not told, as in the *Gospel of Eve,* that the seer stood, as it were, apart from himself, and saw his little self and greater Self simultaneously. He is conscious of a Presence, of a persona in the highest theological meaning of the word, who is not seen so much as felt. He speaks to this Presence mind to Mind; he *hears* this Presence rather than sees it.

THE VISION OF CREATION

The first part of the question he "holds" in his mind is: How came this cosmos into being? The answer is the changing of the Boundless Presence into "Light -- sweet joyous Light." He loses all sight of "all things" in his mind (the mental image he had formed of cosmos) and is plunged into the infinitude of Limitless Light and infinite joy, which transports him out of himself in highest ecstasy.

But he has craved for Gnosis, not joy and light, but Wisdom, the understanding and reconciliation of the great Opposites, the Cross of all Manifestation. Therefore must he know the Mystery of Ignorance as well as that of Knowledge. Within the infinitude of Light appears the Shadow of the Unknown, which translates itself to his consciousness as Darkness -- the Shadow of the Thrice-unknown Darkness -- which, as Damascius tells us, "was the First Principle of the Egyptians, the ineffable Mystery, of which they said nothing," and of which our author says nothing.

This Darkness comes forth from within outwards to the disciple's consciousness, and it spreads "downwards" in sinuous folds like a Great Snake, symbolizing, presumably, the unknown, and to him unknowable, mysteries of the differentiation of the root of matter of the cosmos that is to be. Its motion is spiral, sinuous, unending vibrations -- not yet confined into a sphere; not yet ordered -- but chaotic, in unceasing turmoil, a terrible contrast to the sweet peace of the Light. This primordial darkness gradually changes from Dark Space into a Fluid or Flowing Matter, or Watery Substance. That is, presumably, what the Greek mystics would have called Rhea, the Primal Mother or First Matter of the future universe before it has even been manifested.

It wails and groans -- that is to say, its motion is as yet unharmonized. In the terminology of the Sophia-mythus, it is the inchoate birth from the Sophia Above, in the Fullness, brought forth by herself alone without her syzygy (or consort). On account of its imperfection, she wails and groans to the Father of All and His Perfections, that her Perfection may be sent to fashion her child, who is herself in manifestation, into a world of order, and eventually into Perfection in its turn.

The Primal Undifferentiated or Chaotic Sound, from the Darkness of its first state, gradually manifests itself under the brooding power of the Boundless Light, into less confused thunderings and murmurings, and finally reaches a stage symbolized by the "Cry," which is a Voice of Fire. This is passionate Fire, not distilled Light, and it expresses a need and want, longing for union with the Articulate Power or Cosmic Word.

The three most primal stages thus seem to be symbolized by Fire, the Watery Substance, and Darkness. These were not our differentiated elements but the Primal Pre-cosmic Elements, what Christian theologians would call the Father, the Son, and the Holy Ghost. The same idea, though in different forms, is met with in a system of the Gnosis preserved for us by the Old Latin translator of Irenmus and also by Theodorer who ascribes it to the Sithians, whom he says are also called Ophianae or Ophirae. Now, Seth was Typhon or Darkness, Dark Light, and this Seth may very well have been symbolized as the Great Serpent of Darkness, as it is in our text. Hence the name "Those of the Serpent," perhaps given them by their theological adversaries (orthodox Jews and Christians). In this system the Primal Elements are given as Water, Darkness, Abyss, and Chaos. The Light was the Child of the supreme Trinity -- the First Man, the Second Man, and the Holy Spirit or First

Woman. This Light is what the Jewish and Christian overworking of the original tradition called the Cosmic Christ.

Thus the Fire of Desire, or the Cry in the Darkness, was to be satisfied or checked or quenched by the Light's fashioning its inchoate substance into the cosmos; and so in another Vision, preserved in another treatise in the *Corpus Hermeticum,* Hermes sees "through the gaze of the Master," the cosmos in its finished beauty, when all things in it are full of Light and nowhere is there Fire or Darkness.

FIRST EMANATION: THE DECENT OF THE LOGOS

Upon this Cry for Light, into the Heart of the Dark-Moist-Fiery nature is injected a Holy Word, the Seed of the future Cosmos. This Word is articulate, reasonable, and ordering. The Cosmic Animal Nature is impregnated with the Light of the Supernal Reason, which pervades its whole being. This pervading immediately effects an ordering of the Chaotic Elements into Pure Fire, Pure Air, and Pure Water-Earth. Moreover, it is to be gathered from the sequel that Nature saw the Word and all his beauty in her Fire and Air, but as yet only *heard* him in her Water-Earth.

The Shepherd thus explains that Light is really Mind, and Mind is really God -- God prior to Nature but not prior to Darkness. The Unity of Light and Darkness is a still higher Mystery. Light and Mind is the highest concept the disciple can yet form of God. The Light-Word, or emanation of Supernal Reason, is Son of God, Son of Great Mind.

THE REVELATION OF THE PLEROMA

At this point in the treatise, the sequence of the narrative is broken by a second vision and is only resumed later. The breaking of the main narrative may be regarded as a necessary digression rather than as an interpolation of foreign material. It is necessary in order to bring on to the scene the hitherto invisible Greatnesses, "within" the Veil of Light, which constitute the Economy of the Pleroma. More had to be seen by the disciple before he was in a position to understand what he had so far seen. He must now unite with the Light, his previous seeing being that of its reflection on his own mind. Not that this logos and Light (or Mind) are separate. They are in reality one, the Son is one with the Father in the state that transcends all opposites. The Logos apparently comes forth, yet it remains ever with the Father, and this coming-forth-and-yet-remaining constitutes its Life -- in other words, it is an emanation. Thus Hermes is bidden to understand the Light: as Life, and so make "friends" with it.

Hitherto the Light had been one for him a sameness that his highest vision could not pierce, the Veil of Light that shut the beauties, perfections and greatnesses of the Intelligible from the eyes of his mind. To pierce this veil, a still more expanded power of sight had to be given him by the Master. The little word or lightspark within him is intensified by the Great Word of the Master, this Word being an Intelligible Utterance of the One Mind, an intensification of being.

Hermes now sees and understands the countless Powers within the Light, which constitute the Intelligible Archetypal Forms or Divine Ideas of all worlds. Between the special sensible cosmos of his prior vision and this Immensity was a Mighty Power or Great

Boundary (Horos) that encircled the elements of the sensible cosmos and held its Fire in check.

GOD DESIRING HIMSELF

In amazement, Hermes asks whence come these apparently disorderly and untamed elements of the new world that have to be subdued and separated from the concord of the perfection of the Powers? And the answer is that Chaos, too, has its being from God's Will. Discord and Concord, Chaos and Cosmos, are both of God. The Primal Elements are, as it were, the passions of God's Will desiring Himself. It is Himself as Mother or Spouse desiring Himself as Father. In other of the Trismegistic tractates this "Feminine Aspect" of Deity is called Wisdom, Nature, Generation, or Isis. He is Wisdom as desiring Himself -- that Desire being the Primal Cause as Mother of the whole world-process, which is consummated by His Fullness uniting with His Desire or Wisdom, and so perfecting it. This is the whole burden of the Gnostic Sophia-mythus, from which the main elements of the Pymander might be derived.

The Mother, when thought of as without the Pleroma, is impregnated by the Word, which the Gnostic Basilides would have called the Allseed Potency of the Pleroma endowed with all Powers, and sent forth as the seed of the sensible cosmos that is to be. The Mother in her higher nature contemplates the Eternal Cosmos (or Order of the Pleroma) and in her lower nature copies its beauties by means of the permutations and combinations of her elements and the generations and transformations of her lives or souls.

What some authors have seen as the fundamental dualism of our text is, however, by no means so very marked, for it leaves it clearly to be inferred that the Darkness comes from the Light itself, for previously there was nothing but Light and all thing had become Light to the eye of the seer. It was, in my opinion, precisely for the sake of removing the thought of dualism that the seer is shown a still more intimate vision within the Light Veil, where all ideas of monotheism, dualism, tritheism, polytheism, and pantheism lose their formal distinctions in a Formless State, or, at any rate, in a state of being where all are interblended with all. In describing it, the "tongue of flesh" has to use the familiar language of form, but every word employed has a new significance; for even the "tongue of angels" cannot describe it, or any of the "tongues" of heaven; He alone who speaks forth the Words of the One Mind can express it.

Whence this sublime conception of the Pleroma came, I do not know. It seems to me impossible to find a geographical origin for such things, as, indeed, it seems vain to seek a geographical origin for the primordial dualism and the rest. For the writer of our tractate these ideas came from the nature of things, from the immediate experience of sight. The form of expression, of course, may be susceptible of a geographical treatment, but as yet I am not satisfied that any clear background has been made out for this supposed interpolation. The Feminine Divinity, next the Highest God, is not set over against that God, but is His own Will. He is in the Pleroma Vision as much and as little male and female as in the general narrative. He transcends all opposites and contains all opposites in Himself.

What is clear, however, is that in the combination of both visions we have before us a simple and early form of the Gnosis which we meet with later in Christian overworkings, and especially in the very elaborate expositions of the Basilidian and Valentinian schools, the systems of which can, in their main elements, be paralleled and compared point by point with our treatise; but this would be too lengthy a proceeding in our present study.

SECOND EMANATION: MIND THE MAKER

We now return to the main narrative. Within the World-Egg, which was encircled by the Mighty Power (the Gnostic Horos), there had already been developed the three Cosmic Elements of Fire, Air, and Water-Earth. This had been effected by the descent of the Cosmic Logos into the Primal Elements of Disorder. As the Logos descended, Fire and Air ascended, and the Logos remained in Water-Earth. This was the result of the First Outpouring from the potency of the Pleroma the First Word uttered by the One Mind.

The Second Outpouring of Mind was of Mind no longer regarded as Light only, but as Light and Life, Male-Female. This emanation appeared as the enforming Mind -- that is, Mind the Maker, the Fashioner or Former, Artificer or Demiurge of lives or souls. It was the ensouling of the Ordered Elements of Nature with lives, whereby these Cosmic Elements were drawn together into forms.

The Great Mind, as Light and Life, reflected itself in the "pure formation" of Nature -- that is to say, in Fire and Spirit (Air), Fire for Light and Spirit for Life, to further enform, things. The Mighty Power or Self-limitation of Mind, the boundary that no mortal can pass, marks off the formative area of the whole cosmos. This area, however, was by no means only the mixed sensible world that we perceive with our present physical senses. On the contrary, there are within it various orders of the main cosmos. For the Ordering Mind, as the Enformer or Soul-fashioner, differentiates itself into seven Ruling Forms or Spheres that "enclose" the mixed sensible cosmos; these spheres, therefore, must be of a psychic nature -- that is to say, of a pure or subtle substance. They are forms of subtle matter endowed with reason. They constitute the cosmic engine of the fashioning of souls, or psychic natures, and of their perpetual transforming. Their energies and activities are those of Fate, or the ordered sequence of cause and effect, symbolized by spheres perpetually entering into themselves.

In all the main phases of this divine operation, there is to be observed the idea of a downward tendency followed by an upward. The Darkness descends; it then transmutes itself and aspires above in a Cry, or Vibration, or primordial yearning for Light. The Word descends, and immediately the Fire and Air ascend. Mind the Maker descends, and immediately the Word ascends from the mixed Water-Earth, which unites (at-ones) itself with its co-essential emanation from the Father. This creates a space about the Seven, and thus leaves the still down-tending elements in the Element Water-Earth deprived of its immediate presence, after giving physical matter the initial impulse to order. This physical matter our author calls "pure matter," meaning thereby matter deprived of the immediate presence of Reason.

Hereupon from the impulse she has received, Nature begins her physical enformation, develops her physical elements and bodies of irrational lives. Water-Earth divides into water and earth, and also air, for this air is clearly something different from the Spirit-Air that ascended; the lower air is one of the downward elements.

THIRD EMANATION: THE DESCENT OF MAN

When this had been accomplished, there followed a Third Outpouring -- the descent of Man, the consummation of the whole enformation of things, a still more transcendent manifestation of Mind, the One Form that contains all forms, His Very Image coequal with Himself. God finally becomes Himself to consummate and save the cosmos in the form of Man -- that is, to gather it to Himself and take it back into the Pleroma.

Nevertheless, the Word and the Mind the Maker and Man are not three different persons; they are all co-essential with each other and one with the Father. For the Word is co-essential with the Demiurgic Mind, and the latter is Brother of Man, and thus Man is coequal with God. And so Man, as the Beloved, descends; and in his descent he is clothed with all the powers of his Brother's creative energy, the creative energy of Life conjoined with rational Light.

Having learned the lesson of the conformations and of the limitations of the Spheres, he desires to break right through the Great Boundary itself; but to do this, he must descend still further into matter. Before he can burst through upwards, he must break through downwards. Accordingly he breaks through the Spheres downwards, seeking his consort Nature below, and shows her his Divine Form radiant with all the energies bestowed on him by all the Powers above.

And she in her great love, wound herself round the image of this Form mirrored upon her water, and the shadow of it thrown upon her earth. Just as the Darkness wound itself, like a Great Serpent, round the lower parts of the Light, so does Nature coil herself round the shadow and reflection of Man. Man is Above, yet he is Below; man is free, yet is he bound -- though bound willingly in love for her who is himself.

Some readers are greatly puzzled with all this. It must be noted, at this juncture, that the writer of our treatise did not discover new ideas or invent new terms; he used what was in his mind and the mind of his circle. It was, however, the weaving of it into a whole, not as a literary exercise, but as a setting forth in the most understandable terms with which they were acquainted of the "things seen," that was their main interest. Those who had the "second sight" would understand and appreciate their labors, those who had not would never understand, no matter what terms or what language was used.

In this section of the Pymander, our treatise is endeavoring precisely to give an insight into the state of things beyond Fate. The burden of its teaching is that all earthly duality and oppositions are really illusory; man can transcend these limitations and come into the freedom of the Sons of God. Even the most terrible and fundamental oppositions are not really so, but all are Self-limitations of God's Will. And man is Son of God coequal with Him.

THE FIRST MEN

Our treatise goes on to describe the first appearance of man on earth, which it regards as a great mystery never before revealed ("the mystery kept hid until this day"). This I take to mean that it had hitherto never been written about but had been kept as a great secret. This secret was the doctrine that the first men, of which there were seven types, were hermaphrodites, and not only so, but lived in the air; their frames were of fire and spirit, and not of the earth-water elements. The Celestial Man, or type of humanity, was gradually differentiating himself from his proper nature of Light and Life, and taking on bodies of fire and air, was changing into mind (Lightfire) and soul (Life-spirit).

This presumably lasted for long periods of time, the lower animal forms gradually evolving to greater complexity as Nature strove to copy the "Form" of Man, and Man devolving gradually until there was a union of Mind and matter, and the human subtle form could find vehicles among the highest animal shapes. The first incarnate men appear to have been at first also hermaphrodite; and it must have been a time when everything was in a far greater state of flux than things are now.

TO INCREASE AND MULTIPLY

This period of pre-sexual or bisexual development having come to an end, the separation of the sexes took place. The commandment is given by the Word: "Increase in increasing and multiply in multitude." It is true that this is reminiscent of the oft-repeated formula in Genesis, but it is only slightly reminiscent. The main injunction is similar, but the rest of the Logos being quite different from anything found in Genesis. As nothing else in the whole treatise can be referred to direct Hebrew influence, we must conclude that the formula was, so to speak, "*in* the air," and has so crept into our treatise.

This increasing and multiplying, the perpetual coupling of bodies and the birth of new ones, is effected by Fate, or the Harmony of the Formative Spheres, the Engine of Birth, set under Forethought or Providence. This Pronoia can be none else than Nature herself as the Wisdom or Knowledge of God -- in other words, His Will.

LOVE AS THE WILL OF GOD

The motive power of all this is Love. If this Love manifests itself as Desire for things of matter, the Lover stays in Darkness wandering; if it becomes the Will to know Light, the Lover becomes the Knower of himself, and so eventually at-one with Good. But why should love of body merit Death -- that is to say, make man mortal? The disciple attempts an explanation from what he has seen. Although his answer is approved, the meaning is by no means clear.

The physical body, or body in the sense-world, is composed of the Moist Nature, which in a subsequent phase remains as Water-Earth, and in a still subsequent phase divides itself into the elements of physical earth, water, and air. The dissolution of the previous combination of these elements is effected by Death -- that is, Darkness, the Drainer of the Water, the Typhonean Power. Water must thus here symbolize the Osirian Power of fructification and holding together. The Moist Nature seems to be differentiated from the Darkness by the energizing of Light in its most primitive brooding. But seeing that the Light is also Life, the Darkness, which is posited as the ultimate opposite, must be Death.

THE WAY OF DEATHLESSNESS

The Way of Deathlessness is then considered. The disciple repeats his lesson, and the Master commends him; the Way Up is the path of self-knowledge. Still the disciple cannot believe that this is for him; he cannot understand that the One Mind is in him, or rather is himself, in so much as Mind as Teacher seems to be outside him. The semantic play is on Mind and mind; the one gives the certitude of Immortality, the other is still bound by the illusion of Death. The disciple has not this certitude; the One Mind, then, is not his.

The Master then further explains the mystery. Gnosis must be preceded by moral purification; there must be a turning-away before the re-turn can be accomplished. The whole nature must be changed. That is the alchemy of the cosmos. Every tortuous effort that the little man seems to make of his own striving is really the energizing of the Great Man.

Those, however, who yield themselves to lower desires, drive the One Mind away, find that their appetites are only the more strengthened by the mind in them. The original text of this paragraph is very corrupt, so that the exact sense of the original is not recoverable; and this makes it all the more difficult to understand what is meant by the Avenging Daimon, the Counterpart of the Mind.

THE ASCENT OF THE SOUL

Before long, the subject of instruction becomes the Way Above, or ascent of the soul out of the body at death. The physical body is left to the work of change and dissolution. The life of integration and conservation ceases, and the life of disintegration begins. The form thus vanishes, apparently from the man's consciousness; that is to say, presumably, he is no longer clothed in the form of his physical body but is apparently in some other vehicle. The particular fixed form, or "way of life," or "habit," he wore on earth being handed over to the Daimon deprived of all its energy, so that apparently it becomes an empty shell.

The senses that had previously been united by the mind become separate. That is, instead of a whole they become parts; they return to the natural animal state of sensation, and the animal part of man, or his vehicle of sexual passion and desire, begins in its turn to disintegrate, the mind or reason (logos) being gradually separated from it. Or rather, its true nature begins showing forth in the man, as he gradually strips off the irrational tendencies of the energies. Those irrational tendencies have their sources in Fate (the Harmony of the Spheres) It is in these seven subordinate spheres or zones where he leaves his inharmonious propensities, deprived of their energy. For Fate (the Harmony of the Spheres machine) is only evil apparently; it is really the Engine of Justice and Necessity to readjust the foolish choices of the soul. That is, it exists to purify the soul's irrational desires, or those propensities in it that are not under the sway of the right reason of the One Mind.

THE EIGHTH SPHERE

The soul of the initiated strips itself naked of the "garment of shame," the selfish energizings, and stands "clothed in its own power." This refers probably to the stripping off of the dress of selfhood, the garments woven by its vices, and the putting on of the "wedding garment" of its virtues. This state of existence is called the Eighth, a state of comparative sameness that transcends the zones of "difference." It is the Ogdoad of the Gnostics, the City of Jerusalem Above, the plane of the Higher Ego in its own form, the natural state of "those-that-are."

In another sense, it may perhaps mean that man, after passing through the phases of the lower mind, now enters within into the region of the pure One Mind, the Higher Ego, and there is united (at-oned) with all the experiences of his past lives that are worthy of immortality, his virtuous energizings -- the "those-that-are" that perhaps constitute the "crown of mighty lives" sung of by the Pythian Oracle when celebrating the death of Plotinus.

In this state the man, who has freed himself from the necessity of reincarnation, hears the Song of the Powers above the Ogdoad -- that is to say, in Gnostic terms, the Hymn of the Eons of the Pleroma, the Music of the Spheres. Such a man would have reached the consummation of his earthly pilgrimage and be ready to pass on into the Christ-state, or, at any rate, the state of super-man. He would be the victor who had won the right of investiture with the Robe of Glory, and the dignity of the crowning with the Kingship of the Heavens. This final initiation is most: beautifully set forth in the opening pages of the *Pistis Sophia*, and especially in the "Song of the Powers," beginning with the words: "Come unto us, for we are thy fellow-members. We are all one with thee."

The consummation of the mystery is that the alter-egos of the individual ego, or the sum total of purified personalities that in that state constitute its membership (or vehicles of their own selves) surrender themselves to a fullness of union or a transcendency of separation, in which they become the powers or energies of a New Man, the true Son of Man. They pass into a state where they each blend with all, and yet lose nothing of themselves, but rather find in this new union the consummation of all their powers. In this state of Sonship of the Divine, they are no longer limited by bodies, nor even by partial souls or individual minds; but, becoming Powers, they are not only in God, but one with the Divine Will. In fact, in the final consummation, they are God Himself.

Of such a nature was the Shepherd Hermes; he, too, was the Christ of God, the Son of the Father, who could take all forms to carry out the Divine Will. When the form -- even though that form might for the disciple take on the appearance of the cosmos itself, as he conceived it -- had served its purpose, the Shepherd once more "mingled with the Powers."

THRICE-GREATEST HERMES

The Shepherd Hermes was known as Thrice-Greatest, which described both his states of consciousness and the bodies in which he manifested. That trinity is carried forth in most modern religious and spiritual traditions. The Shepherd's name was Christ for those who prefer the name of the Christian tradition, or Buddha for those who are more familiar with Eastern terms. For instance, the so-called "three bodies" (*trikayam*) of the Buddha suggest he manifested on three levels not just earthly individuality. Buddhahood, like Christhood and Hermes, is a state beyond individuality in the separated sense in which we understand the term. In all three cases, the first step to existing in higher states is getting beyond the confines of one's individuality. In the Chinese Version of Ashvaghosha's now lost Sanskrit treatise, *Mahajana-Shraddhotpada-Shastra* we read: "It is characteristic of all the Buddhas that they consider all sentient beings as their own self, and do not cling to their individual forms. How is this? Because they know truthfully that all sentient beings as well as their own self come from one and the same Suchness and no distinction can be established among them."

The sentient beings who do not obtain Buddhahood or Christhood do not know that their Body of Transformation is merely the shadow (or reflection) of their own evolving consciousness. They imagine it comes from some external sources, and so they give it a corporeal limitation. But the Body of Transformation really has nothing to do with limitation or measurement. That is to say, a Buddha can only communicate with such minds by means of a form, that form being really that of their own most highly evolved consciousness. There are, however, others who have the consciousness of the "formless" state, but have not yet reached the Nirvanic Consciousness. These in Buddhism are called Bodhisattvas.

We have used the term "formless state" to signify the states of consciousness in higher worlds but these are only "formless" for consciousness that has not reached the Bodhisattva level. For this Body of Transformation has infinite forms and each form has infinite attributes. Each attribute has infinite excellencies. And the accompanying reward of Bodhisattvas -- that is, the region where they are predestined to be born -- also has infinite merits and ornamentations. Manifesting itself everywhere, the Body of Bliss is infinite, boundless, limitless, unintermittent, directly coming forth from the One Mind. An older Chinese version of the Sanskrit treatise quoted above says of this Body: "It is boundless, cannot be exhausted, is free from the signs of limitation. Manifesting itself wherever it should manifest itself, it always exists by itself and is never destroyed."

In other words, one who has reached the Nirvanic Consciousness -- that is to say, the Master -- can teach or be active on "planes" that are as yet unmanifested to us ordinary folk; these "planes", however, even when the disciple is conscious of them, are conditioned by the self-limitation of his own imperfection. The vehicles of this activity are called by various names in different spiritual traditions (Dharmakaya, Astral Body, the Wedding Garment) and the limitation of their activity is determined on the side of the disciple by the degree of his ability to function consciously in those states that are known in theosophical nomenclature as those of Atman, Buddhi, and the Higher Manas, or, in more general terms, those of the divine, spiritual, and human aspects of the self.

In the first degree of conscious discipleship, then, the Master communicates with His disciples and teaches them by means of the human body. He quickens the highest form of consciousness or conception of masterhood they have so far attained to, taking the form of their greatest love, perhaps, as they have known Him in the flesh, or as He has been told of as existing in the flesh, but not His true form, which would transcend their consciousness. The next stage is when the disciple learns to transcend his own egoity in the ordinary sense of the word; this does not mean to say that his true individuality is destroyed, but instead of being tied down to one ego-vehicle he has gained the power of manifesting himself wherever and however he will, at any moment of time. In brief, he has attained the power of self-generation on the plane of egoity in that he has reached a higher state that is free from the limitations of a single line of egoity.

The disciple now begins to realize in the very nature of his being that the "Self is in all and all in the Self." Such a disciple (or Bodhisattva) is taught by the Master in this state of being, and the body that he supplies for the energizing of his beloved Father is perfectly unintelligible to us, and can only be described as an expanded consciousness of utmost sympathy and compassion, which not only strives to blend with the life of all beings but also with the One Being in the world for him, the "Beloved." Such a sensing of the Master's Presence is called the Body of Bliss.

There is a still higher Perfection, the Own Nature of Masterhood, the "I Am that I Am" state. But how should the dim mind of one who is outside imagine the condition of One who is not only Within, but who combines both the Outside and the Within in the Transcendent Unity of the Perfect Fullness?

THE SPREAD OF THE GNOSIS

With the consummation of the higher teaching and the return to earth of the consciousness of the Seer, our treatise breaks off into a graphic instruction of how the new Gnosis is to be utilized. The Wisdom is no man's property; he who receives it holds it in trust for the benefit of the world. Until this point, we have moved in the atmosphere of an inner intimate personal instruction, set forth in a form evidently intended only for the few. Indeed, as we find in other treatises emphatic injunctions to keep the teaching secret, we cannot but conclude that such a revered and authoritative document of the Hermetic school was at one time guarded with the same secrecy.

In any case, all things are new for our author; all things have new meanings. He has become a Son of God, instead of a procession of Fate; he has reached the "Plain of Truth." In Christian terms, the Christ has been born in *his* heart consciously. Henceforth his effort will be to become like unto the Father Himself, to pass from Sonship into the Perfection of perfection, Identity or At-one-ment with the Father.

THE MEANING OF "PYMANDER"

Many researchers have already remarked that the name "Pymander" is formed irregularly in Greek, and this has led to an interesting speculation by Frederick Granger in his commentary where he writes: "While, however, the name Pymander does not answer to any Greek original, it is a close transliteration of a Coptic phrase. In the dialect of Upper Egypt 'py-meretre' means 'the witness'. That the Coptic article (py) should be treated as part of the name itself is not unusual. Such a title corresponds very closely in style with the titles of other works of the *Corpus Hermeticum*, such as *The Perfect Word*, which is an alternative title of the "Asclepius." The term Pymander, therefore, on this supposition, contains an allusion to the widely spread legend of Hermes as the witness, a legend that is verified for us from many sources. Nonetheless, the meaning taken in most commentaries is that of "the Good Shepherd," in the sense of Hermes, the Shepherd of Man. This was certainly the idea conveyed to the non-Egyptians by the name, however philologically unsound its form may be.

It has been no part of our task to attempt to trace the Hermes idea, for this would have led us too far from our immediate subject. There is, however, one element of that tradition which is of great interest, and to which we may draw the attention of the reader in passing. The beautiful idea of the Christ as the "Good Shepherd" is familiar to every Christian child. *Why* the Christ is the Shepherd of all men is shown us by this first of the marvelous treatises of the *Corpus Hermeticum*. In it we have the universal doctrine apart from any historical dogma, the eternal truth of an ever-recurring fact, and not the exaggeration of one instance of it.

The representation of Christ as the Good Shepherd was one of the earliest efforts of Christianity, although the prototype was far earlier than Christianity. In fact, it was exceedingly archaic. Statues of Hermes as the Kriophoros, or Hermes with a ram or lamb standing beside him, or in his arms, or on his shoulder, were one of the most favorite subjects for the chisel in Greece. We have specimens dating to the most archaic period of Greek art. Hermes in these archaic statues has a pointed cap and not the winged headdress and sandals of later art. This type in all probability goes back to Chaldean symbolic art, to the bearers of the twelve "signs of the zodiac" and the "sacred animals" of the stars. These were, in one human correspondence, the twelve "septs" or classes of priests. Here we see that the Greek tradition itself was not pure Aryan even in its so-called archaic period. Chaldea had given her wisdom to post-diluvian Greece, even as she had perchance been in relation with Greece before the Great Flood.

CONCLUSION

Here, then, we have another element in the Hermes idea. In fact, nowhere do we find a pure line of tradition; in every religion there are blendings and have always been blendings. There was unconscious syncretism (and conscious also) long before the days of Alexandria, for unconscious syncretism is as old as our race-bindings. Even as all men are kin, so are popular cults related; and even as the religion of nobler souls is of one paternity, so are the theosophies of all religions from one source.

One of the greatest secrets of the innermost initiated circles was the grand fact that all the great religions had their roots in one mother soil. And it was the spreading of the consciousness of this stupendous truth that subsequently gave rise to the many conscious attempts to synthesize the various phases of religion, and make "symphonies" of apparently contradictory philosophical tenets. Modern research, which is essentially critical and analytical, and rarely synthetical, classifies all these attempts under the term "syncretism" -- a word that it invariably uses in a depreciatory sense, as characterizing the blending of absolutely incompatible elements in the most uncritical fashion. But when the pendulum swings once more towards the side of synthesis, as it must do in the coming epoch -- for we are but repeating today in greater derail what happened in the early centuries -- then scholarship will once more recognize the unity of religion under the diversity of creeds and return to the original doctrine of the Hermetic Mysteries.

www.ingramcontent.com/pod-product-compliance
Lightning Source LLC
LaVergne TN
LVHW041503070426
835507LV00009B/776